SOLDIERS
OF THE FIRST
WORLD WAR

VOICES FROM THE
TRENCHES

SIMON ADAMS

FRANKLIN WATTS
LONDON • SYDNEY

First published in 2013 by Franklin Watts

Copyright © Franklin Watts 2013

Franklin Watts
338 Euston Road
London NW1 3BH

Franklin Watts Australia
Level 17/207 Kent Street
Sydney, NSW 2000

A CIP catalogue record for this book is available from the British Library.

Dewey no: 940.3

Hardback ISBN: 978 1 4451 2380 6
Library eBook ISBN: 978 1 4451 3072 9

Printed in China

Franklin Watts is a division of Hachette Children's Books, an Hachette UK company.

www.hachette.co.uk

Editor: Sarah Ridley
Editor in Chief: John C. Miles
Designer: Jason Billin
Art Director: Peter Scoulding
Picture Research: Diana Morris

Picture credits: Gary Blakely/Shutterstock: 42br. Ernest Brooks/Hulton Archive/Getty Images: front cover bg. Ernest Brooks/Imperial War Museum: 15t. Chrislophotos/Shutterstock: 43cl. Lt.Adrian Duff/Corbis: 39c. Sgt Morris Fineberg/Corbis: 40b. Christel Gertenberg/Corbis: 7. The Granger Collection/Topfoto: 6t, 12t, 29t. greatwar.nl: 21b. Hulton Deutsch/Corbis: 11t, 34. Lightroom Photos/Topfoto: 37b. Mirrorpix:1b, 16t, 16b,18c,27t,28t,28b,31,33b,39b. PA/Topham: 41b. Picturepoint/Topham: 13b, 26, 36, 37c. Print Collector/HIP/Topfoto: 14c, 24. Roger-Viollet/Topfoto: 9b, 30bl, 40c. Maurice Savage/Alamy: 25b. Christopher Seidler/ Franklin Watts: 1c, 13t, 20cr, 42tr. Stapleton Historical Coll/HIP/Topfoto: 30br. Topfoto: 5, 18b, 19, 32, 33c, 35, 38. Topical Press/Getty Images: 6b, 10b, 11b, 15b. Ullsteinbild/Topfoto: 8, 12b, 17b, 25c, 29b. Wikipedia Commons: front cover r,42bl.

Every attempt has been made to clear copyright. Should there be any inadvertent omission please apply to the publisher for rectification.

Note to parents and teachers

Every effort has been made by the Publishers to ensure that the web sites in this book are suitable for children, that they are of the highest educational value, and that they contain no inappropriate or offensive material. However, because of the nature of the Internet, it is impossible to guarantee that the contents of these sites will not be altered. We strongly advise that Internet access is supervised by a responsible adult.

CONTENTS

THE GREAT WAR

In 1914 war broke out in Europe and soon spread around the world. Millions of soldiers, sailors and airmen were killed or injured during the next four years. This terrible war became known as the Great War, but after a second world war broke out in 1939, the Great War was renamed the First World War.

Archduke Franz Ferdinand and his wife minutes before they were assassinated in 1914.

Why the war happened

The war was caused by events in Europe. The most powerful countries had formed two large alliances to defend themselves against attack. When a Serb assassinated the heir to the Austro-Hungarian throne, Archduke Franz Ferdinand, in Sarajevo, Bosnia on 28 June 1914, Austria-Hungary blamed Serbia and declared war. Russia supported its friend Serbia, Germany supported Austria-Hungary against Serbia and Russia, and France supported Russia against Germany and Austria-Hungary. When the German army invaded Belgium in order to attack France, Britain and its empire joined the war on the side of its French and Russian allies.

The first battles of the war were fought between the professional armies of the countries involved. Reservists were called up and thousands of men rushed to enlist to serve their country.

Fritz Kreisler, officer in the Fourth Battalion, Third Army Corps, Austro-Hungarian army

1 August 1914

We went by way of Munich. It was the first day of the declaration of the state of war in Germany. Intense excitement prevailed. In Munich all traffic stopped; no trains were running except for military purposes. ...

We reached Vienna on August first. A startling change had come over the city since I had left it only a few weeks before. Feverish activity everywhere prevailed.... Motorcars filled with officers whizzed past. Dense crowds surged up and down the streets. Bulletins and extra editions of newspapers passed from hand to hand. ... Of course, the army was idolised. Wherever the troops marched the public broke into cheers and every uniform was the centre of an ovation.

Personal accounts

Many millions of men fought in this war. Fighting abroad for long periods of time, they wrote letters and cards to their loved ones and friends back home. Some kept diaries of their time in the army. Many of them also spoke later about their experiences during the war. It is these letters, diaries and personal statements – most of them from the Western Front – we look at in this book. Through them, we can begin to understand what it was like to have fought in the Great War.

Rifleman Burton Eccles, 7th (S) Battalion, The Rifle Brigade, British army, writing to his mother from France

Easter Sunday, 1917

Well Mother Darling, I must close now. I do not expect to be able to write field cards even, for a day or so. But do not worry about that. I am fit and well and as soon as I can, I will write you a letter. Please tell my little sweetheart that I wished to write to her today but could only get one letter off. You must let her see this letter.

A British soldier snatches a few minutes to write a letter home.

WHEN WAR BROKE OUT

Although tensions had been building between nations in Europe, war broke out quite suddenly in the summer of 1914. A shooting in Sarajevo in the Balkans at the end of June that people thought little about quickly led to fighting across Europe in August.

An unexpected war

The outbreak of war took many people by surprise. Most young men had jobs to go to and lives to lead. They were confused and bewildered, as they did not know what war would mean for them.

Times

AUGUST 5, 1914   1 D.

BRITAIN AT WAR

In London, bank holiday crowds reacted to the latest news about the outbreak of war.

Newspaper headlines gave readers the fateful news.

Private Reginald Haine,
1st Battalion, Honourable Artillery Company, British army

August 1914

My first reaction to the outbreak of the war was more or less a blank, because I did not really think much about it. I was only just eighteen, and right at the start I didn't think that it would affect me to any extent. I was an articled clerk to a firm of chartered accountants and I was due for a fortnight's holiday. I went on that holiday on August the 4th [the day war broke out].

Over by Christmas?

Men on both sides quickly joined the army. They were proud to fight for their country and thought that victory would come quickly. Many people thought that the war would be over by Christmas 1914. Others thought it might take a little longer. They were all wrong, as the war was to last another four years.

Most young men, such as these employees hard at work in a factory in Hanover, Germany, had settled jobs. They didn't know what war would mean for them.

Sergeant-Major Paul Fontanille, 6th Chasseurs Alpins, French army

August 1914

Tears when we said goodbye. Personally, I'm not at all apprehensive, but who knows what the future holds. There are lots of rumours doing the rounds already. The war's going to last a fortnight etc. Myself, I reckon two months at least.

CONSCRIPTION

Lieutenant Henri Desagneaux, French army, writing in his diary

1–4 August 1914

From the early hours Paris is in turmoil. The banks are besieged. At last at 4.15 in the afternoon, the news spread like wild-fire, posters are being put up with the order for mobilisation on them! It's every man for himself, you scarcely have time to shake a few hands before having to go home to make preparations for departure. At six in the morning after some painful goodbyes, I go to Nogent-le-Perreux station. ...

When the war started the French people all went crazy. I remember all along the Boulevard Haussmann from the Opera House to the Place de la République there were thousands of men and women marching up and down shouting, 'à Berlin! à Berlin!'
They were shouting all night long.

In most European countries except for Britain, young men were forced by law to serve in the national army for a period of at least two years. These men then served in the reserves until they were too old to fight. When war broke out, the army and all its reserves were mobilised for action.

Mobilisation

Mobilising an army involved getting together and organising hundreds of thousands of men. Full members of the armed services returned quickly to their regiments. Conscripts and reservists received call-up papers summoning them to fight. Supplies and munitions were got ready, and weapons prepared.

Young German men cheer as they prepare to join the army.

**Corporal Stefan Westmann,
29th Division, German army**

August 1914

I was a medical student when I received my call-up papers. They ordered me to report for military duty in a clean state and free of vermin at an infantry regiment in Freiburg.

We had no idea of any impending war. We had no idea that the danger of war existed. We served in our blue and red uniform, but on the 1st of August mobilisation orders came and we put on our field grey.

**Lieutenant Fritz Nagel,
Reserve Field Artillery Regiment
No. 18, German army**

On August 4, 1914, I presented myself to the army as a reservist and was told I now belonged to the Reserve Field Artillery Regiment Nr. 18, which was forming in Bahrenfeld near Hamburg.

Relatives were not allowed near the building where we had to assemble. As soon as I could, I gave a message to a little boy so my family knew I would be shipped out to Bahrenfeld within the hour.

Uncertain future

For some men, mobilisation came as a nasty surprise. They had never fought in the army before, and did not know what to expect. They did not even know which regiment they would be placed in.

French men form a queue outside a temporary military office.

A group of recently mobilised French soldiers stand in front of their tents.

KITCHENER'S ARMY

Unlike the other major countries fighting in 1914, Britain's professional army was made up of volunteers. No one was forced to fight against their will at this stage. Soldiers signed up for a period of seven years in the army plus a further five in the reserves.

"Your Country Needs YOU"

The British Secretary for War was General Kitchener, a famous war hero. He realised that the regular army was not big enough to fight the Germans successfully. He therefore appealed for 100,000 volunteers to sign up. Thousands immediately responded to his appeal. Many joined local Pals' battalions, organised on a local basis so that the new recruits had their 'pals', or friends, with them in the army.

The power of this recruitment poster, showing General Kitchener pointing at the viewer, motivated thousands of young men to enlist.

New recruits pledge their loyalty to king and country.

Private Thomas McIndoe,
12th Battalion, Middlesex Regiment,
British army

Autumn 1914

It was seeing that picture of Kitchener and his finger pointing at you – any position that you took up the finger was always pointing to you – it was a wonderful poster really.

Under age

Some young men were so keen to enlist that they lied about their age. The minimum age was 18. However many joined much younger. The huge losses suffered by the army meant that there were still not enough recruits of any age to fight. In 1916, conscription was introduced: all single men aged 18 to 41 were forced to enlist.

New recruits formed long queues outside army recruiting offices.

London street children dress up as soldiers in November 1914 and pose in front of a huge poster to try and convince more men to join the army.

THE NEED FOR FIGHTING MEN URGENT.

Private Thomas McIndoe, 12th Battalion, Middlesex Regiment, British army

Autumn 1914

When I confronted the recruiting officer he said that I was too young, although I had said I was eighteen. He said, 'Well, I think you are too young, son. Come back in another year or so.' I returned home ... I picked up my bowler hat, which ... was only to wear on Sundays. I presented myself to the recruiting officer again, and this time there were no queries. I was accepted. ... I was sixteen in the June.

GETTING INTO UNIFORM

Once they had joined the army, the new recruits were sent to a training camp. Here they learned to fight. Army life was a new experience to all of them, but they quickly adapted to their new existence.

New recruits

In the camp, the new recruits trained to become soldiers. They exercised to improve their fitness. They learned how to handle and fire a gun. Some learned about signals and communications. Everyone learned drill, the repetitive carrying out of orders on the parade ground that teaches soldiers how to obey commands. This gave soldiers the discipline they would need in battle.

Learning how to load and fire a rifle was an important part of army training. These young British recruits are not yet in uniform.

Private F B Vaughan, 12th Battalion, York and Lancaster Regiment, British army

Autumn 1914

... we had a will of our own and it came rather hard to start to obey commands, but gradually we knew how to form fours, right wheel, left wheel, and all the rest of them. We became in other words a disciplined body of men and then the training consisted largely of route marches. Then we learned how to excavate the ground and make trenches ...

Fixing bayonets is one of the most wonderful things in the Army. The sergeant-major was telling the troops how to fix arms, how to fix bayonets, and he said, 'When I says fix, you don't fix, but when I says bayonets you whips 'em out and whops 'em on.'

These German recruits are using sacks filled with straw for bayonet practice.

New uniforms

Putting on military uniform for the first time made the recruits realise that they were now proper soldiers. The uniforms were often uncomfortable but necessary, as they protected the soldier from the elements and identified which regiment he belonged to.

A young German non-commissioned officer poses proudly for the camera in his new uniform.

New recruits to the British army, being measured up for their uniform. This consisted of a khaki tunic and trousers, a shirt, belt, pair of boots, a service cap, a greatcoat or overcoat and a backpack. In 1916 the cap was replaced by a steel helmet.

Lieutenant Fritz Nagel, Reserve Field Artillery Regiment No. 18, German army

6 August 1914

On August 6 I was issued my field grey uniform which I had never worn before. The colour was grey-green with dull buttons, the helmet was covered with a grey cloth so the ornaments would not glitter in the sun and the high riding boots were brown and very heavy. The whole outfit was heavy and ill-fitting.

GOING TO THE FRONT

Once the training was over, the soldiers left their barracks and training camps and went off to fight. Many soldiers had never left their home towns before. Most had never gone abroad in their lives.

Marching to war

Most new soldiers went to war after only a few weeks of training. They were unused to carrying heavy equipment and found the army regime difficult to accept. The front line of the war was often many kilometres away, so the new soldiers had to march for days.

Fritz Kreisler, officer in the Fourth Battalion, Third Army Corps, Austro-Hungarian army

August 1914

We proceeded to Graz, where we joined the other three battalions and were entrained for an unknown destination. ... It must be understood that the only reports reaching us from the fighting line at that time were to the effect that the Russians had been driven back from our border, and that the Austrian armies actually stood on the enemy's soil. ...

This first day's march constituted a very strong test of endurance in consequence of our comparative softness and lack of training, especially as, in addition to his heavy rifle, bayonet, ammunition, and spade, each soldier was burdened with a knapsack containing emergency provisions ... On top of this heavy pack a winter overcoat and part of a tent were strapped, the entire weight of equipment being in the neighbourhood of fifty pounds.

Members of the British Expeditionary Force disembark from their ship at a French port in 1914.

Many German troops travelled to the front by train.

Going abroad

Going abroad was a new experience for most troops. Troops from the British Empire travelling from Australia, Canada, India, New Zealand, the West Indies and South Africa had long sea journeys. Troops from the French Empire also travelled long distances. Many soldiers were homesick.

Soldiers of the British West Indies regiment cleaning their rifles in France, 1916.

William Henry Dawkins, Australian army engineer, writing home to his mother from Egypt

26 December 1914

Yesterday was Christmas Day and our thoughts were in Australia. ... some of my section had the most gorgeous dinner ... They said that they only had to shut their eyes and they could imagine they were home again.

A few weeks later, he wrote again

28 February 1915

I received your letter dated 26 January during the week and it may be the last I receive in Egypt as we are moving shortly. To where no one knows. ...
I tip the Dardanelles as our destination but it may be anywhere in France, Turkey, Syria or Montenegro. Anyway it is a move and at last we will be getting to work.

Australian troops, carrying their kit, disembark from a troop ship.

THE TRENCHES

Most wars are mobile affairs, with armies advancing and retreating over long distances and battles fought along the way. This was not true in the First World War. In Western Europe, the Allies and the Germans opposed each other along a line of static trenches that stretched from the English Channel south through Belgium and France to the Swiss border.

Lines of trenches

The Allied and German trenches ran for 760 kilometres, facing each other across a narrow gap known as no-man's land. Each line consisted of a front line trench for fighting, a support line to supply the front line with food and weapons, and a reserve trench at the rear. The lines ran in zig-zags, with communication trenches between them. The trenches were dug at speed and were often very wet and uncomfortable. The same was true for other trenches dug on the Eastern Front with Russia and at Gallipoli in the Ottoman Empire (modern Turkey).

Belgian troops dig trenches in September 1914.

Sergeant W H Lench, 1st Newfoundland Regiment, Newfoundland army, remembering the trenches at Gallipoli in the Ottoman Empire

November 1915

I posted the sentries and walked up and down the trench. … Everywhere I moved I stumbled over dead bodies … I crawled through water with two men after me. I got within 20 yards of the Turks' wire on my first patrol. I saw them digging in the darkness, improving their trenches and putting up new wire.

Cavalry cross a bridge built over a trench, with troops passing underneath.

German trenches

German trenches were better constructed than the Allied ones. Their trenches were built to last, as the Germans were defending territory they had captured from the enemy. German trenches were reinforced with wood and often had shuttered windows, floorboards and even doormats. Occasionally, a German trench was captured and became home to Allied soldiers.

German trenches were generally very deep and had semi-permanent structures inside.

Lieutenant Richard Talbot Kelly, Royal Artillery, British army

1915

I went along the communication trench and slipped over the side into this German trench. It was very impressive. To begin with, the Germans had run short of sandbags when they had built their trenches in this part of the world, and they had looted the cottages round about and made sandbags out of curtains, counterpanes and every other material they could lay their hands on. So these trenches were the most varied and coloured affairs you could imagine, and faded wonderfully into the wildflowers and cabbages and everything else of the landscape – in fact they produced a camouflage excellence that we never achieved again in the war.

ARMY RATIONS

An army consumes a huge amount of food and other essential supplies. Soldiers received daily rations but were always grateful for parcels of food and other items sent from home.

Feeding the troops

The French emperor Napoleon Bonaparte said that "an army marches on its stomach". The armies that fought in the First World War were no exception. Provisions were brought up to the front, often by railway, and then cooked in the trenches and on the front line. The meals were dull and the cooking often poor.

Lieutenant Jacques Meyer, 329th Infantry, French army

1915

The main meal of the day was stew. Called soup, it contained poor quality meat, forming a rubbery magma with pasta or rice, or perhaps beans, more or less cooked, or potatoes, more or less peeled, [all] in a sort of thin gruel ...There was no question then of vitamins or green vegetables.

Canadian troops eat a meal at the front line. The grave of one of their comrades lies just behind.

Indian troops cook naan (flatbread) on a griddle to go with their meal.

Fritz Kreisler, officer in the Fourth Battalion, Third Army Corps, Austro-Hungarian army

September 1914

This distribution of food had now become a formidable task, in consequence of the unforeseen movements and diversions which were forced upon us by the unexpected developments of the battle; and it often happened that food supplies intended for a certain detachment would reach their destination only after the departure of that detachment.

Parcels

Families sent out parcels of food and extra clothing to their sons at war. These gifts were very welcome and often replaced army rations. Some troops, however, received surprises when they opened the post. In January 1916 a British sergeant major put on a new pair of socks and found a packet of cigarettes inside with this message attached:

Dear Soldier,

Soon these socks will be worn out. When you want another pair, write to

Miss Meta Kerr

Mulagh

Islandmagee

Ireland

A merry Christmas and a safe return.

MK

The arrival of the post was eagerly awaited, as it brought welcome letters and sometimes gifts from home.

PREPARING FOR BATTLE

Life on the Western Front could be dull. Days went by without any fighting, with only the occasional artillery bombardment to keep everyone alert. And then, all of a sudden, an order went out to get ready to fight.

German Mauser rifle bayonet. Soldiers fixed bayonets to their rifles for hand-to-hand fighting.

A quiet day in a front-line trench. A sentry keeps watch while other soldiers sleep.

In readiness

Soldiers were prepared to fight at any time, as an enemy surprise attack could quickly overwhelm them. They never knew when they might have to advance or go out on a mission, as orders were kept secret until the last possible moment. This created high levels of stress for soldiers.

Lance-Sergeant Frank Wilfrid Watts, 15th Battalion, London Regiment, British army, writing memories of Vimy Ridge, France, in 1929

21 May 1916

I was on camp-cleaning fatigue, but, the camp being in good condition, there was nothing to do beyond picking up an odd piece of paper or two. After dinner, most of the men settled down in huts to sleep or write letters; it was all very pleasant and happy, something like Sunday at home. ... About five o'clock we sat down to tea. In my hut we had just drawn our rations when the company commander appeared at the door and said in a strange voice, 'Pack up immediately! Pack up immediately!' We swallowed our tea, put on our equipment and fell in outside. In half an hour the battalion was on the road, marching in the direction of the line. When we met the other companies it was obvious from the faces of officers and men that something serious was afoot.

"Prepare to move"

The greatest fear was the order to prepare to go over the top, that is to leave the trenches and go out across no-man's land to capture an enemy trench. Perhaps only one in four men would survive unharmed, the rest being wounded or killed. Every soldier was afraid of what was about to occur.

British troops prepare to go over the top to attack enemy lines. The soldier on the right is using a trench periscope to see above the top of the trench.

Private Fred Ball, King's Regiment (Liverpool), British army, writing about the Battle of the Somme in 1929

27-28 July 1916

I remember the first night when I was called upon to go over the top ... we were told to be prepared to move into the line that night... All through that night I never had a wink of sleep. My stomach would insist on rising to my throat to choke me each time I thought of some lurid possibility. And so the night passed and we remained where we were.

In the morning we were told that our affair had been postponed twenty-four hours. ... Last night we thought we were going over the top. Tonight we know. Our CO himself has told us. Back come all the bogies of the previous night. I find myself engaged in calculating the chances of escape. Surely a quarter of our number will remain unscathed. I have one chance in four of coming out none the worse. ... And so I tortured myself that second night.

A remarkable colour view of no-man's land, as seen from a French fortified position.

UNDER BOMBARDMENT

Before an army advanced on foot, its artillery sent a massive barrage of shells raining down on the enemy trenches. These barrages sometimes went on for days. Their aim was to destroy the enemy's trenches so that they could be taken with minimal loss of life.

Planned bombardment

An artillery barrage was carefully planned. Heavy artillery, such as howitzers, pounded the trenches and any defensive earthworks to kill enemy soldiers and destroy machine guns, while lighter field artillery tried to flatten the fences of barbed wire strung across no-man's land to protect the enemy's trenches. The barrage was incessant, produced by soldiers who worked in shifts throughout the day.

Lieutenant W E Walters-Symons, Royal Garrison Artillery, British army, remembering the lead-up to the Battle of the Somme

Last week of June 1916

The initial softening bombardment, for the battle of July the 1st, extended over a period of seven days. In a howitzer battery we were given daily programmes for the destruction of earthworks, and portions of trenches which had to be carefully ranged on, and subsequently annihilated. ... All [enemy trenches] had to be dealt with, trench junctions demolished and a general annihilation of the area in which the enemy was living.

The task was carried out each day and meanwhile, while the heavier guns were annihilating earthworks, the field artillery were busy cutting the dense wire protecting the German front line, endeavouring to cut paths for our assaulting infantry at zero hour. We fired about 800 to 1,000 rounds per day, the equivalent to many tons. It took twelve men to man an 8-inch howitzer, the shell of which weighed 200 lb, and the preservation of manpower necessitated careful reliefs which took place every four hours.

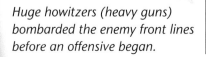

Huge howitzers (heavy guns) bombarded the enemy front lines before an offensive began.

Clouds of earth fly up into the sky as Allied artillery shells explode near German trenches.

Massive artillery bombardments left behind a devastated landscape.

Under fire

Living inside a trench under artillery fire was dangerous and terrifying. The noise was deafening and damage to the trenches immense. Soldiers were in great danger, but they had to remain in the trenches to defend them when the barrage stopped and the enemy infantry began their attack.

Lieutenant Stefan Westmann, 29th Division, German army, remembering the lead-up to the Battle of the Somme

Last week of June 1916

For a full week we were under incessant bombardment. Day and night, the shells came upon us. Our dugouts crumbled. They would fall on top of us and we'd have to dig ourselves and our comrades out. Sometimes we'd find them suffocated or smashed to pulp. Soldiers in the bunkers became hysterical – they wanted to run out, and fights developed to keep them in the comparative safety of our deep bunkers. Even the rats became hysterical and came into our flimsy shelters to seek refuge from the terrific artillery fire.

For seven days and seven nights we had nothing to eat and nothing to drink while shell after shell burst upon us.

BLOWING UP THE LINES

Soldiers fought not just on the ground but also below it, laying mines that would explode under enemy lines. One famous event took place at Messines Ridge near Ypres in Belgium in June 1917.

Digging under

On 7 June 1917 the British army planned to capture German positions on a ridge near Messines. To do this, they used teams of British, Canadian, Australian and New Zealand miners to dig a series of trenches and tunnels that stretched 5,453 metres to finish deep under the German lines. They then dug and filled 25 mines with explosives. The work was dangerous, as the tunnellers were under constant German bombardment.

Tunnellers dug deep under enemy lines so that explosives could be laid and detonated.

Private E N Gladden, 7th Battalion, Northumberland Fusiliers, British army, writing in 1929

5 June 1917

On the morning of June 5th I was awakened from a deep sleep – I had been out carrying bombs until the early hours of the morning – and ordered to join the party detailed to assist the Australian Tunnelling Company, who were working day and night in six-hour shifts.

The sergeant in charge of the party conducted us down a labyrinth of passages more marvellous at every step, until we came to an opening to the outer world. ... We moved round a corner in the breastwork and formed a continuous chain to transport the bags [of earth] back into the galleries where they were wanted for tamping – that is, for building a barrier against the backward force of the explosion. ... Suddenly the [German] gun fired again and something in the scream of the first shell foretold that it was for us. I ducked as it burst opposite the corner of the breastwork. We ran like rabbits for the sap [side trench].

The big bang

The 25 mines were filled with more than 450 tons of high explosives. At 03:10 hours on 7 June, 19 of the mines were successfully exploded. The blasts, which were heard 100 kilometres away on the south coast of England, blew away the top of the hill and all the German positions on it. More than 10,000 German soldiers died instantly in the explosion. The British quickly seized the ridge.

Sapper Roll, 1st Australian Tunnelling Company, Australian Engineers

7 June 1917

The whole hillside rocked like a ship. The noise from the artillery was deafening and the thunder from our charges was enormous. The infantry dashed forward under the barrage and kept sending back thousands and thousands of prisoners. They came back through our dugouts and they were absolutely demoralised. We were all so happy we didn't know what to do! Then, when we got to look at the craters, we saw there were lumps of blue clay as big as small buildings lying about. Our Hill 60 crater was a hundred yards across from lip to lip and forty-five yards deep, although a lot of the stuff had naturally fallen back into the crater. We thought the war was over.

The successful explosion of the mines under Messines Ridge created huge craters in the landscape.

The craters of Messines Ridge are still visible today. This one is now a large pond.

OVER THE TOP

Leaving the safety of the trenches and going 'over the top' of the parapet into no-man's land was the most dangerous thing a soldier could do. Once there, he was exposed to constant enemy gunfire.

Into the fire

The bombardment of enemy trenches was meant to wipe out all their machine gunners and destroy all the fortifications, but unfortunately, this rarely happened. Many soldiers found themselves heading straight into enemy gunfire.

British troops run towards the remains of the barbed wire protecting the enemy trenches.

Infantryman in the 258th Brigade, French army, describing the opening day of the Second Battle of Champagne

25 September 1915

At the appointed hour, the officers gave us the usual pep talk, a few final instructions, then asked if we were ready. A moment's silent contemplation followed our positive reply; then suddenly someone shouted 'Advance.' ... We scrambled onto the next parapet and ran towards the first wave, shouting whatever came into our heads: 'Vive la France!' 'Death to the Boches!' 'Come on boys!' The guns were rattling away in front of us ... We caught up with our friends now but – to our horror – met a barbed wire barrier that was still intact and more than thirty metres deep. And all this time the enemy machine-guns carried on, rat-tat-tat, while to right and left we could see our comrades falling, strewing the ground with their blue uniforms, red with blood where they'd been hit.

Moving barrage

One tactic employed was for troops to advance just behind a moving barrage of shells. As the artillery barrage crept forward, so too did the troops. This tactic sometimes worked quite well, but many enemy troops still survived this bombardment to resist the advancing troops.

German storm troopers crouch in a forward trench waiting for their artillery barrage to finish before going over the top.

Lieutenant W E Walters-Symons, Royal Garrison Artillery, British army, remembering the first day of the Battle of the Somme

1 July 1916

Assaulting troops . . . left their trenches and walked up to within 150 yards of the barrage as formed on the ground. At zero hour the barrage proceeded into the enemy line in steps of 100 yards at a time. The assaulting troops followed the barrage and on reaching the enemy front-line trench descended into it and had hand-to-hand battles with the occupants.

The barrage crept forward and the assaulting troops followed it until the support line was reached, when similar hand-to-hand fighting took place. The barrage then crept at a slow rate of 100 yards per minute to the extent of the gun range. . . .

Unfortunately, during the heat of the attack the German troops had not been mopped up out of their deep dugouts, some of which were 20 to 25 feet deep. They recovered from the initial shock, came up into the trenches and quickly established fire.

IN BATTLE

A battlefield was not a neat and tidy place. The ground was muddy and churned up by the artillery bombardment. The air was full of smoke. Soldiers were under fire from almost every direction and often lost their sense of direction.

Firing blind

During the course of a battle, bursts of gunfire ran out across the battlefield. Gunners often fired blind, for if they looked out of the trench or stopped to locate the enemy, they risked getting shot. The noise was immense, and the battle often chaotic.

Machine-gun teams under fire by the side of a road.

Canadian troops dug into a sea of churned-up mud at the Battle of Passchendaele, 1917.

Fritz Kreisler, officer in the Fourth Battalion, Third Army Corps, Austro-Hungarian army, under fire from the Russians in Galicia

September 1914

We marched on until the command was given for us to deploy, and soon afterwards the first shrapnel whizzed over our heads. It did no harm, nor did the second and third, but the fourth hit three men in the battalion in the rear of us. ... The next shell burst right ahead of us, sending a shower of bullets and steel fragments around. A man about twenty yards to the right of my company ... leaped into the air with an agonising cry and fell in a heap ... Then came in rapid succession four or five terrific explosions right over our heads, and I felt a sudden gust of cold wind strike my cheek as a big shell fragment came howling through the air.

Stretcher-bearers at Passchendaele carry a wounded soldier through the knee-deep mud of the battlefield.

Private H Baverstock, 1st Canterbury Battalion, New Zealand Division, remembering the Battle of the Somme

July 1916

At that moment, a sledge-hammer hit me just above the left knee. I crashed onto my face and my military career came to an abrupt and painful end. ... Any movement was agony, and I had to lie there trying to endure it.

I suppose the time was about 2 o'clock on the Saturday afternoon. After a few hours, two stretcher-bearers ... found me and dragged me quite a distance to the sunken road. ... Having done all they possibly could for me, they told me they would have to return to Flers to get the stretcher.

Whether those two brave Medical Corps chaps were killed I could not say, for I never saw them again. ... There I lay for about two days. ...

At long last, early on the Monday morning, two other stretcher-bearers found me and lifted me onto their stretcher. ... The whole battlefield was strewn with the bodies of New Zealanders killed ... and not yet buried.

The fallen

Fighting stopped for many soldiers as soon as they got injured. They lay where they fell, waiting for a lull in the battle to allow stretcher-bearers to come and retrieve them and carry them to safety for medical care. Some had to wait days. Others soon died; their bodies were eventually retrieved and buried.

After a battle, the dead lie unattended on the battlefield before their bodies are collected.

INVALIDED OUT

In the course of the war, more than 21 million soldiers were seriously injured. For many of them, the fighting was over, but they faced a different challenge – to regain their health. Some had to learn to cope with a life-long disability.

Medical care

An injured soldier received medical attention at a first-aid post, close to the front line, before he was taken to a dressing station in one of the rear trenches. If his injuries were severe, he was moved by horse-drawn or motor-powered ambulance to a casualty clearing station about 10 kilometres from the front. The seriously wounded were transferred to a military hospital and eventually to hospitals in their home country for treatment or for convalescence.

Xavier Chaïla, 8th Cuirassiers, French army, remembering the first day of a major French offensive against the Germans along the Aisne River

16 April 1917

We picked up a number of wounded men to carry them to the rear. It was no small matter trying to get down blocked communication trenches ... We had to go as far as the canal ... There were at least 400 seriously wounded men on the banks. The chief medical officer was fuming. Although this attack had been planned for a long time, no provision had been made for the evacuation of the wounded ... It was the Boche [German] prisoners who had to carry the stretchers over a considerable distance. Some of our wounded had to spend forty-eight hours on the canal bank, in the rain, the cold, and the shell-fire. Many of them died there because they couldn't be treated in time.

Medical orderlies treat an injured soldier in a trench while (above) the wounded lie on stretchers at a casualty clearing station further behind the lines.

Far from the front line, wounded soldiers help each other at a large military hospital.

A 'Blighty wound'

Blighty was the name British soldiers gave to Britain. Some soldiers hoped to get a 'Blighty wound', a wound that was serious enough to send them back home but not bad enough to kill them.

Corporal Clifford Lane, 1st Battalion, Hertfordshire Regiment, British army

Winter 1916

What I had felt under shellfire, especially during the first two years, was a wish for a wound, a 'Blighty wound' we called them, to get me home. You thought a Blighty wound was the most fortunate thing that could happen to you.

But there were times, after being shelled for hours on end during the latter part of the Somme battle, that all I wanted was to be blown to bits. Because you knew that if you got wounded, they could never get you away, not under those conditions. You'd see other people with internal wounds and you thought your only hope was to get killed outright, your only relief. It wasn't only me who felt like that, it happened to lots of people.

GAS ATTACK!

Both sides in the war used toxic gas against enemy troops. At first, the gas was thrown in grenades and canisters. Later, it was fired in shells in a liquid form that evaporated on impact.

Gassed, by war artist John Sargent. He witnessed a mustard gas attack at Ypres in 1918. The gas burnt the skin, caused temporary blindness and made it very difficult to breathe.

The use of gas

The first use of gas was by French troops, who used tear-gas grenades against advancing German troops in France in August 1914. Chlorine gas was first used on the Western Front at Ypres in Belgium on 22 April 1915. French Algerian troops, known as Zouaves, noticed a grey-green gas cloud floating towards them from the German lines. They panicked and ran, because they had no protection against the deadly chlorine gas.

Private W Underwood, 1st Canadian Division, Canadian army, at Ypres in Belgium

22 April 1915

Then we saw coming towards us the French Zouaves. They were in blue coats and red pants and caps and it was a revelation to us, we hadn't seen anything but khaki and drab uniforms. They were rushing toward us, half staggering, and we wondered what was the matter. ... They were running away from the Germans. ... Then, as we looked further away we saw this green cloud come slowly across the terrain. It was the first gas that anybody had ever seen or heard of, and one of our boys, evidently a chemist, passed the word that this was chlorine.

Sergeant Jack Dorgan, 7th Battalion, Northumberland Fusiliers, British army at Ypres

26 April 1915

We'd only gone a hundred yards in front of the Canadians when we encountered the gas. We'd had no training for gas prevention, never heard of the gas business. Our eyes were streaming with water and pain, and all we had was a roll of bandages in the first-aid kit we carried in our tunic. So we bandaged each other's eyes. And anyone who could see would lead a line of half a dozen or so men, each with his hand on the shoulder of the one in front. In this way lines and lines of British soldiers moved along, with rolls of bandages around their eyes, back toward Ypres.

Killing gases

Many different types of gas were used: mustard gas was feared the most, as it could attack the skin through normal clothing. Gas was first felt on the face but then quickly entered the nose and throat, causing the victim to cough and choke. Some gases caused temporary blindness, while others flooded the lungs with liquid. About 1,200,000 soldiers were gassed at some point, of whom at least 90,000 died.

Soldiers wore goggles to keep the gas out of their eyes and padded masks to protect their nose and throat.

Deadly gas swirls around Scottish soldiers, who are wearing their gas masks during a battle.

Carlos Diez, a soldier in one of the predominately Basque regiments of the French army on the Western Front

September 1915

The Germans used gas, [causing] panic in the trenches. Despite our masks, which greatly impeded our view, we continued to move forward by walking over the dead and wounded. ... I couldn't breathe and thought my end had come.

REFUSING TO FIGHT

Some young men had strong political and religious objections to the war and refused to sign up. Others turned against the war, once they had experienced it, refusing to fight or obey orders. Both groups were brave men facing impossible circumstances.

More than 16,000 British men became conscientious objectors during the war. This group was imprisoned at Dyce Camp, near Aberdeen.

CONSCIENTIOUS OBJECTORS TO MILITARY SERVICE DYCE CAMP.

Howard Marten, a British conscientious objector court-martialled and sentenced to 10 years in prison for refusing a military order

1916

Our ranks [of objectors] ... were made up of men from every conceivable walk of life. ... They had a terrible repugnance of war.

One or two of the officers and NCOs were quite reasonable men. There was a little Scottish regimental sergeant-major, and he almost had tears in his eyes. He said, 'You don't know what you're up against. You'll have an awful time.' He was genuinely concerned at the trouble we were going to meet.

We were forever being threatened with the death sentence. ... It was all done with the idea of intimidating us. But we wouldn't have taken that line unless we were prepared to face that situation, we realised that it was sufficiently serious.

Conscientious objectors

Men not wearing military uniform were often given white feathers by people who thought they were cowards. Some were soldiers who were off-duty at the time, wearing normal clothes. Those who refused to fight because of their beliefs – many were pacifists and would never fight a war – were known as conscientious objectors, or 'conchies'. Some eventually agreed to do work of national importance such as farming while others performed non-combat duties such as carrying stretchers in the trenches. A few refused all types of service and were sent to prison.

All armies in the war shot soldiers who deserted or refused to obey orders.

Corporal Henri Floch, 298th Infantry, French army, shot for desertion at Vingré near Soissons in northern France

3 December 1914

By the time this letter reaches you, I will be dead. Here's why. On 27 November, around five in the evening, after a violent two-hour barrage over our front line, and just as we were finishing our meal, the Germans got into our trenches and took me prisoner, along with two of my colleagues. I took advantage of a bit of confusion to escape German hands. I followed my comrades and was then accused of abandoning my post in the presence of the enemy. Twenty-four of us appeared yesterday evening in front of a court martial. Six of us, including me, were condemned to death.

Deserters

Once in uniform, some men were completely terrified by the battle going on around them and could not fight. They were often suffering from a reaction to heavy bombardment known as shell shock. Some refused to obey orders and tried to run away. Three hundred and six British and Empire troops and 236 French troops were shot for desertion. A few soldiers in the French army were shot for desertion merely 'for the sake of example'.

TAKEN PRISONER

Throughout the war, about 8 million men were taken prisoner by the other side. International law stated they had to be well treated, but many were forced to work hard and were often cold and hungry.

Hands up!

As the advantage in a battle swung from one side to the other, it was easy for groups of soldiers to get surrounded and taken prisoner. The most dangerous time occurred when they first met the enemy: one false move or misunderstanding and they could be shot dead.

As the war progressed, thousands of German prisoners were taken. They had to be held securely in camps.

Vizefeldwebel [Staff Sergeant] Haftmann, 9th Company Reserve Infantry Regiment 107, German army, fighting at Champagne in France

16 February 1915

With shouts of 'Hurra!' and the throwing of grenades over the obstacle, we had soon closed up to it. ... Horror-struck and totally demoralised by the effect of our grenades, the French cowered behind the barricade and ceased to defend themselves. There was an instant reply to my shout of 'Hands up!' ... About fifteen prisoners remained in my hands.

Corporal Sidney Amatt, 7th Battalion, Essex Regiment, British army, captured during the German offensive into France

March 1918

We were given instructions to retire. ... Next thing, we heard a German voice up above. One of the chaps with us who knew a little German said he's calling down that we've got to surrender. ... We were ordered to come up with our hands up. ... When we got to the top of the trench I was astonished to find the whole area we'd occupied a few hours before was swarming with Germans.

British prisoners of war sit under guard in a railway wagon on their way to a German prisoner-of-war camp.

In captivity

Once in captivity, prisoners often had to work hard. Some were treated harshly, others were well looked after. All suffered acute boredom, as they wanted to escape and get home.

German prisoners of war behind barbed wire in England.

AMERICA JOINS THE WAR

German attacks on American shipping and its hostile moves to encourage Mexico to attack the United States led the USA to join the war on the Allied side on 6 April 1917. Large numbers of American troops joined the fighting in Europe in May 1918.

New troops

The arrival of American troops in Europe was greeted everywhere with much celebration by the Allies. The American troops were fresh and strong. Above all, they were keen to fight, although they quickly had to be trained in the art of trench warfare and acquire other new skills.

Private John Figarovsky, 1st US Division, US army

1918

When we landed, one of the first things we did was to parade through the town of St Nazaire. The French people were just delirious with joy, because in the Americans they saw hope for the future. As we marched through town, the sidewalks and even the gutters on both sides were full of people – and we felt so proud and important that such a fuss was being made over us. The mayor even proclaimed a holiday.

When we trained with the French, they were very cooperative. ... But they were very nonchalant about everything. I guess they were tired after four years of warfare. And they were surprised to see that we were so eager to get into the fight.

During 1918 large numbers of American troops disembarked in France and headed off to fight at the front.

Major Hartwig Pohlmann, 36th Prussian Division, German army

July 1918

In July 1918 we tried to cross the River Marne, but after three days we had to fall back. The resistance of the enemy was just too heavy. We also met the first American troops and we saw from month to month more and more American troops would come to the front line. The enemy became overwhelming for us. But we knew that we had to do our duty as soldiers. It was a matter for the politicians to find a way to a fair peace. So we did our duty as long as we could and most of the German soldiers did so. We had very heavy losses in that year, and units became smaller and smaller. We were forced to form one company out of two, and so on. The number of our guns diminished and so we had to fall back from one line to another.

The American army had no tanks of it own, and so used this lightweight French Renault FT tank and heavier British tanks.

The American effect

A total of 2,084,000 American troops arrived in Western Europe during 1918. Led by General John Pershing, their arrival in such large numbers helped the Allies push the Germans back towards their own country, and eventual defeat.

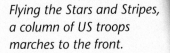

Flying the Stars and Stripes, a column of US troops marches to the front.

THE END OF THE WAR

A massive German offensive into France in March 1918 was halted by the Allies in August. The Allies then took the offensive and pushed the Germans back home. As Germany's allies left the war, Germany itself began to collapse. On 11 November an armistice was agreed that ended the war.

German military leaders (left) prepare to sign the Armistice agreement on 11 November.

Sergeant T Grady, US Army, on the Western Front

11 November 1918

Cold and raining. Runner in at 10.30 with order to cease firing at 11.00 am. Firing continued and we stood by. 306th Machine-Gun Company on my right lost twelve men at 10.55, when a high explosive landed in their position. At 11.00 sharp the shelling ceased on both sides and we don't know what to say. Captain came up and told us that the war was over. We were dumbfounded and finally came to and cheered – and it went down the line like wildfire.

The Armistice

The Armistice was signed between German and Allied leaders in a railway carriage in the forest of Compiègne in northern France and came into effect at 11 am (12 pm German time) on 11 November 1918. Fighting continued right up to the last minutes. Then the guns fell silent across Europe, and peace returned to the world for the first time in more than four years.

American troops in France celebrate the end of the war at 11am on 11 November 1918.

Greeting the peace

The peace was greeted in different ways. Crowds celebrated on the streets of London, Paris and elsewhere but most soldiers in the field were too exhausted to celebrate. For the Germans, defeat now stared them in the face.

The royal family greet the celebrating crowds outside Buckingham Palace.

Gunner B O Stokes, 13th Battery, New Zealand Field Artillery, remembering Armistice Day in northeast France

11 November 1918

We moved on 11 November ... and we heard the announcement of the Armistice when we were still in the Forest de Mormal on a cheerless, dismal, cold misty day. There was no cheering or demonstration. We were all tired in body and mind, fresh from the tragic fields of battle ... We trekked out of the wood on this dreary day in silence. We read in the papers of the tremendous celebrations in London and Paris, but we could not bring ourselves to raise even a cheer. The only feeling we had was one of great relief.

FOR VALOUR

The war created many heroes. Men fought with great bravery for their country and were awarded medals for distinguished service. All were praised for having fought in the toughest of wars.

The Victoria Cross

Each country had its own award for valour, bravery. The highest British military decoration for valour in the face of the enemy is the Victoria Cross. During the war, 628 Victoria Crosses were awarded to British and Empire troops, nine of them for bravery on the first day of the Battle of the Somme on 1 July 1916. French soldiers received the Légion d'honneur, Germans the Iron Cross and Americans the Medal of Honor. All servicemen received war service medals.

From left: the British War and Victory medals and the German Iron Cross.

The Victoria Cross was awarded for acts of extreme bravery in the face of the enemy.

Lance Corporal Walter Peeler, 3rd Battalion, Australian army (left), awarded a VC for his actions during the Battle of Broodseinde

4 October 1917

I never saw the faces of those I killed. They were just men in an enemy uniform. It was simply them or me. I don't think I was brave – not any more than the other Aussies who were with me. I simply had a job to do, and I did it ... Only afterwards did I realise how lucky I'd been not to get killed myself.

Returning home

After the war was over, soldiers returned home to their towns and villages. Some were still fit and healthy. Others were seriously injured. They were all welcomed home as heroes. Many were presented with certificates, just like the author's grandfather. Those that did not return were buried in distant cemeteries and remembered by name on local war memorials.

The Western Front is lined with the cemeteries of fallen soldiers from both sides in the war.

Certificate presented to the author's grandfather on his return from the war by the parishioners of Tidenham in Gloucestershire, England.

General Herbert Plumer, commander of the British Second Army at Ypres, unveiled the Menin Gate dedicated to British and Empire soldiers who died at Ypres and whose graves were unknown

24 July 1927

One of the most tragic features of the Great War was the number of casualties reported as "missing, believed killed". ... To their relatives there must have been added to their grief a tinge of bitterness and a feeling that everything possible had not been done to recover their loved one's bodies and give them reverent burial ... [This] memorial has been erected ... and now it can be said of each one in whose honour we are assembled here today: "He is not missing; he is here."

KEY DATES

1879 Germany allies with Austria-Hungary

1894 Russia allies with France

1904 Britain and France form alliance

1907 Britain and Russia form alliance

1914

28 June Archduke Franz Ferdinand of Austria-Hungary assassinated by a Serb in Sarajevo

28 July Austria-Hungary declares war on Serbia

30 July Russia supports Serbia and mobilises army

1 August Germany declares war on Russia; France mobilises army

3 August Germany declares war on France

4 August German troops enter Belgium; Britain declares war on Germany

22 August First British troops land in France

23 August Austro-Hungarians attack Russians from Galicia

26–30 August Germans defeat Russians at Tannenberg

5–9 September German advance into France halted at the Marne

November Allies and Germans begin to dig trenches along the Western Front

1915

22 April Inconclusive Battle of Ypres begins in Belgium

25 April Allied troops land in Gallipoli in Ottoman Empire

23 May Italy enters war on Allied side and attacks Austria-Hungary

22 September Allies launch unsuccessful attack at Loos in France

1916

21 February Germans begin to attack French at Verdun

31 May Inconclusive naval battle at Jutland in North Sea

1 July British attack Germans at the Somme in France

1917

12 March Revolution in Russia; Tsar Nicholas II overthrown

6 April USA enters war on Allied side

31 July Allied assault begins at Passchendaele in Belgium

6 November Bolsheviks seize power in Russia

1918

3 March Germany and Russia agree peace deal at Brest-Litovsk

7 August German advance into France halted at the Marne

21 August Allies push back Germans

30 September Bulgaria leaves the war

30 October Ottoman Empire leaves the war

3 November Austria-Hungary leaves the war

11 November Allies sign armistice with the Germans; the war ends

1919

28 June Treaty of Versailles signed between the Allies and Germany; further treaties end war with Austria, Bulgaria and Ottoman Empire

FIND OUT MORE

BOOKS

World War I by Simon Adams (Dorling Kindersley, 2001)

World War One: Causes and Consequences, War in the Trenches, Weapons and Warfare, Women and War – four books by Simon Adams, Adrian Gilbert & Ann Kramer (Franklin Watts, 2014)

Brothers at War: A First World War Family History by Sarah Ridley (Franklin Watts, 2013)

The Usborne Introduction to the First World War by Ruth Brocklehurst and Jenny Brook (Usborne, 2007)

My First World War by Daniel James (Franklin Watts, 2010)

PLACES TO VISIT

Imperial War Museum, London

National Army Museum, Chelsea, London

National Maritime Museum, Greenwich, London

The Tank Museum, Bovington Camp, Dorset

The Cenotaph, Whitehall, London

Tomb of the Unknown Warrior, Westminster Abbey, London

Almost every town and village in Britain, as well as many churches, has a memorial to those who lost their lives in the First World War.

There are numerous cemeteries and memorials along the line of the Western Front in Belgium and northeast France.

USEFUL WEBSITES

BBC schools site:

www.bbc.co.uk/schools/worldwarone/

BBC history site:

www.bbc.co.uk/history/worldwars/wwone/

BBC trench virtual tour:

www.bbc.co.uk/history/worldwars/wwone/launch_vt_wwone_trench.shtml

Multimedia site:

www.firstworldwar.com/

US site about the war:

www.socialstudiesforkids.com/subjects/worldwari.htm

GLOSSARY

adjutant Officer in the army who acts as an administrative assistant to a superior

alliance Formal agreement, often military, between two or more nations

Allies, the Britain, France, Russia, Italy and later the USA, who fought on the same side in the war

ally A country that supports another

armistice An agreement between opposing sides to cease fire while a peace settlement is reached

artillery Heavy guns, such as mortars, howitzers and so on, used to bombard an enemy line

Balkans, the Region of southeast Europe, including Serbia, Bulgaria and Romania

Boche, the Slang term for the Germans

Central Powers Germany, Austria-Hungary, the Ottoman Empire and Bulgaria, who fought together in the war

chlorine Gas used in weapons

conscientious objector A person who opposes the war and will not fight for political or religious reasons

CO Commanding officer

conscript Person who is enrolled compulsorily for military service

court-martial Trial of a member of the armed forces charged with breaking military law

dressing station First-aid post in the trenches

empire Large area of land made up of different countries ruled by one nation and its emperor

enlist Enter the armed services

field artillery Lighter artillery weapons

front/front line An area where two opposing armies face each other

grenade Small bomb filled with explosive or gas, thrown by hand or fired from a rifle

heir Legal successor to a person or throne

howitzer Artillery weapons designed to fire a heavy, slow shell with a high trajectory or flight-path

infantry Soldiers who fight on foot

khaki Dull yellowish-brown military uniform

latrines Outdoor toilets

Lewis gun British light machine-gun

mobilise To prepare an army for war; a general mobilisation includes all the armed services and many civilian services

munitions Military equipment and stores, in particular ammunition

no-man's land Unoccupied strip of land between the opposing enemy trenches

padre An army chaplain or minister of religion

rations Army food

recruit Someone who joins the army voluntarily

regiment Basic military unit of up to 1,000 soldiers, often responsible for recruitment and training and organised by region or by military specialism

reserves Members of the armed services not in active service

sapper Soldier who digs trenches or, in the British army, a member of the Royal Engineers

shell Hollow artillery projectile filled with high explosives, shrapnel or liquid gas

shell shock Physical and mental reaction by a soldier to heavy bombardment, causing him to suffer a breakdown

shrapnel Fragments of a shell or the small pieces of metal packed inside a shell that explode on impact

sign up Sign the forms to join the army

treaty Formal agreement between two or more countries

trench Long, narrow and deep ditch in the ground where soldiers lived and fought on the Western Front

valour Great bravery in battle

Victoria Cross Highest British military decoration for valour 'in the face of the enemy' first awarded by Queen Victoria in 1856

volunteer Someone who freely agrees to join the army and fight

Western Front The front line between the Allied and German forces that stretched from the English Channel south through Belgium and France to Switzerland

Zouaves French army soldiers raised in Algeria

ACKNOWLEDGMENTS

The soldiers' words in this book are taken from the following sources:

Imperial War Museum Sound Archive interviews: Sidney Amatt (9168/28), Jack Dorgan (9253/34), Reginald Haine (33/6); Clifford Lane (7257/11), Thomas McIndoe (568/8), Howard Marten (642/8)

'The Great War', BBC TV series, 1964: Interviews with John Figarovsky, Richard Talbot Kelly, Hartwig Pohlmann, Sapper Roll, W Underwood, F B Vaughan, W E Walters-Symons

Gerald Burgoyne: *The Burgoyne Diaries*. Thanks to Thomas Harmsworth Publishing: Letter from MK in Ireland

Peter Englund: *The Beauty and the Sorrow*. Profile Books, London, 2011: Letters from William Henry Dawkins

Fritz Kreisler: *Four Weeks in the Trenches*. Houghton Mifflin, Boston and New York, 1915

Lyn Macdonald: 1914–1918: *Voices and Images of the Great War*. Michael Joseph, London, 1988: Extracts by H Baverstock, Burton Eccles, T Grady, B O Stokes

Fritz Nagel: Fritz: *The World War I Memoir of a German Lieutenant*, ed. Richard A Baumgartner. Blue Acorn Press, Huntingdon, West Virginia, 1995, p 35

C. B. Purdom: *Everyman at War: Sixty Personal Narratives of the War*. J M Dent & Sons, London & Toronto, 1930: Extracts by W H Lench, Frank Wilfrid Watts, Fred Ball, E N Gladden

Jack Sheldon: *The German Army on the Western Front 1915*. Pen & Sword Books, Barnsley, 2012: Extract by Vizefeldwebel Haftmann

Stephen Snelling: *VCs of the First World War: Passchendaele 1917*. The History Press, Stroud, 1998: Extract by Walter Peeler

Ian Sumner: *They Shall Not Pass*. Pen & Sword Books, Barnsley 2012: Extracts by a French infantryman, Xavier Chaïla, Carlos Diez, Henri Floch, Paul Fontanille, Jacques Meyer

Every attempt has been made to contact the copyright holders of quoted materials. Should any references have been omitted, please contact the publisher, who will endeavour to correct the information in subsequent editions.

INDEX